CATHOLIC

■

PRAYERS

LITURGY
TRAINING
PUBLICATIONS

ACKNOWLEDGMENTS

Excerpt from Luke 11 from the *New American Bible with Revised New Testament,* copyright © 1986, 1970, Confraternity of Christian Doctrine, Inc. Washington, D.C. Used by permission. All rights reserved.

Other scripture passages are taken from the *New Revised Standard Version,* copyright 1989, Division of Christian Education, National Council of the Churches of Christ in the United States of America.

Psalm texts are adapted from the *New Revised Standard Version,* and first appeared in *Psalms for Praise and Worship,* copyright 1992, Abingdon Press. Used by permission.

Gospel canticle texts translated by Gail Ramshaw and Gordon Lathrop.

Pentecost Sequence translated by Peter Scagnelli.

Unless otherwise noted, prayers are reprinted from *Catholic Household Blessings and Prayers,* copyright 1988, United States Catholic Conference, Washington, D.C. All rights reserved.

The prayer on page 84 is excerpted from the *Order of Christian Funerals,* copyright 1989, International Committee on English in the Liturgy, Inc. All rights reserved.

This book was compiled and the prayers were annotated by David Philippart, with assistance from Elizabeth Anders. It was designed by Kerry Ishizaki and Anne Fritzinger. Audrey Novak Riley was the production editor. Anne Fritzinger typeset it in Galliard. *Catholic Prayers* was printed by Printing Arts Chicago.

CATHOLIC PRAYERS copyright © 2000, Archdiocese of Chicago: Liturgy Training Publications, 1800 North Hermitage Avenue, Chicago IL 60622-1101; 1-800-933-1800; fax 1-800-933-7094; e-mail orders@ltp.org. All rights reserved.

Visit our website at www.ltp.org.

Library of Congress Catalog Card Number 00-102065

ISBN 1-56854-349-2

CATH

03 02 01 00 99   5 4 3 2 1

JESUS·WAS·PRAYING
IN·A·CERTAIN·PLACE,
AND·AFTER
HE·HAD·FINISHED,
ONE·OF·HIS·DISCIPLES
SAID·TO·HIM,
"LORD,
TEACH·US·TO·PRAY."

—*Luke 11:1*

A NOTE ON THE ART

The image on the cover is by William Morris, one of the leaders of the Arts and Crafts movement. This movement, which emerged just before the turn of the last century, was a return to quality and simplicity after the excesses of the Victorian era. It generated a new respect for the applied arts, such as furniture design and graphic design. One of the hallmarks of William Morris's work was the use of floral patterns, symbolizing a return to nature. This trend led to the flowing lines and stylized plant forms of the Art Nouveau period. The typographical illustrations throughout the book draw from these styles.

Prayer in a Book?

There is an ancient rite called "the presentation of the Lord's Prayer" in which those to be baptized listen as the gathered church speaks these beloved words. Then they are expected to learn it from their sponsors, and return before Easter and speak those same words to God in the presence of the community. This is how we learn to pray: from one believer to another, not from a book!

Yet a prayer book can remind us that our tradition gives us powerful and lovely words with which to give God thanks and praise, to plead when in need and cry out in lament, at morning, noon and night, in sickness and at the dinner table.

And remember that prayer is more than words: It is also singing and keeping still, standing, kneeling, prostrating, bowing, stretching out your hands, lifting up your arms, raising your eyes, intending firmly, seeking sincerely, and ultimately loving deeply. Pray all ways! Pray always!

THE SIGN OF THE CROSS

*The sign of the cross is the first prayer and the last:
of each day, of each Christian life. It is a prayer
of the body as much as it is a prayer of words.
When we are presented for baptism, for the first
time the community traces this sign on our bodies.
Parents may trace it daily on their children. We
learn to trace it daily on ourselves and those we
love. And when we die, for the last time our loved
ones will trace this holy sign on us.*

In the name of the Father, and of the Son,
and of the Holy Spirit. Amen.

In Latin:

In nomine Patris, et Filii, et Spiritus Sancti.
Amen.

HALLOWED
BE·YOUR·NAME.
YOUR·KINGDOM
COME.
YOUR·WILL
BE·DONE.

THE LORD'S PRAYER

THE LORD'S PRAYER

This English translation, first prepared for King Henry VIII at the time of the Protestant Reformation in the 16th century, is based on the longer form of the prayer found in the Gospel of Matthew, chapter 6. There is difficulty with the contemporary meaning of the word "temptation," used here. God never tempts us. The original sense is better expressed in the translation on the facing page: "Save us from the time of trial."

Our Father,
    who art in heaven,
    hallowed be thy name;
    thy kingdom come;
    thy will be done on earth as it is in heaven.
Give us this day our daily bread;
    and forgive us our trespasses
    as we forgive those who trespass against us;
    and lead us not into temptation,
    but deliver us from evil. Amen.

*This is a translation for use among all
Christians.*

Our Father in heaven,
  hallowed be your name,
  your kingdom come,
  your will be done,
  on earth as in heaven.
Forgive us our sins
  as we forgive those who sin against us.
Save us from the time of trial
  and deliver us from evil.
For the kingdom, the power,
  and the glory are yours,
  now and forever. Amen.

This shorter version of the Lord's Prayer is found in the Gospel of Luke, chapter 11.

Father, hallowed be your name,
    your kingdom come.
Give us each day our daily bread
    and forgive us our sins,
    for we ourselves forgive
      everyone in debt to us,
    and do not subject us to the final test.

In Latin:

Pater noster, qui es in caelis:
sanctificetur nomen tuum;
adveniat regnum tuum;
fiat voluntas tua,
sicut in caelo, et in terra.
Panem nostrum quotidianum da nobis hodie;
et dimitte nobis debita nostra,
sicut et nos dimittimus debitoribus nostris;
et ne nos inducas in tentationem;
sed libera nos a malo. Amen.

MEAL PRAYERS

*Before the meal, while making the sign of the
cross on yourself:*

Bless us, O Lord, and these your gifts
which we are about to receive
through your bounty,
through Christ our Lord. Amen.

*After the meal, again while making the sign
of the cross:*

We give you thanks for all your gifts,
almighty God,
living and reigning now and forever. Amen.

I FEAST
AT·A·RICH·TABLE,
MY·LIPS·SING
OF·YOUR·GLORY.
ON·MY·BED
I·LIE·AWAKE.

MORNING PRAYERS

MORNING PRAYERS

*From the Liturgy of the Hours, the daily prayer
of the church, comes this version of two verses
from Psalm 51. It is customary to trace the sign
of the cross on your lips as you pray these words
at the beginning of the day.*

O Lord, open my lips,
and my mouth shall declare your praise.

This psalm is sung at morning, giving thanks for dreaming and for waking. Everything we do this day we do because we crave God.

Psalm 63

O God, you are my God, I seek you,
  I thirst for you;
My flesh faints for you,
  as in a dry and weary land where no water is.
So I have looked upon you in the sanctuary,
  beholding your power and glory.
Because your steadfast love is better than life,
  my lips will praise you.
So I will bless you as long as I live;
  I will lift up my hands and call on your name.

My soul is feasted as with marrow and fat,
    and my mouth praises you with joyful lips,
when I think of you upon my bed,
    and meditate on you in the watches of the night;
for you have been my help,
    and in the shadow of your wings I sing for joy.
My soul clings to you;
    your right hand upholds me.

But those who seek to destroy my life
    shall go down into the depths of the earth;
They shall be given over to the power of the sword,
    they shall be prey for jackals.
But the monarch shall rejoice in God;
    all who swear in God's name shall glory;
    but the mouths of liars will be stopped.

WE·WORSHIP·YOU,
WE·GIVE·YOU·THANKS,
WE·PRAISE·YOU
FOR·YOUR·GLORY!

This ancient hymn of praise, used in the Mass on Sundays and solemn feast days, is of ancient origin. It was known as a psalmoi idiotikoi, *because it sounds like a psalm but is not found in the Bible. The first two verses are the song that the angels sang at the birth of Christ (Luke 2:14).*

Glory to God

Glory to God in the highest,
    and peace to his people on earth.
Lord God, heavenly king,
    almighty God and Father,
    we worship you,
    we give you thanks,
    we praise you for your glory.
Lord Jesus Christ, only Son of the Father,
    Lord God, Lamb of God,
    you take away the sin of the world:
    have mercy on us!
You are seated at the right hand of the Father:
    receive our prayer!

For you alone are the Holy One,
    you alone are the Lord,
    you alone are the Most High,
Jesus Christ,
    with the Holy Spirit
    in the glory of God the Father. Amen.

*This canticle is found in the Gospel of Luke,
chapter 1. It was sung by the priest Zechariah
when his son John the Baptist was born. The
church sings it at the break of day, looking
eagerly for the coming of that dawn from on
high, God's day of peace.*

The Song of Zechariah

Blessed are you, O Lord, the God of Israel!
You have come to your people
    and set them free.
You have raised up for us a horn
    of deliverance
in the house of your servant David.
Through the mouth of
    your holy prophets of old
you promised liberation from our enemies,
    from the hands of all who hate us.
You promised to show mercy to our forebears
    and to remember your holy covenant.
This was the oath you swore
    to our father Abraham:

that, rescued from the hands of our enemies,
    we are free to worship you without fear,
holy and righteous in your sight
    all the days of our life.

You, my child, shall be called the prophet
    of the Most High,
for you will go before the Lord
    to prepare the way,
to give God's people knowledge of salvation
    by the forgiveness of their sins.
In the tender compassion of our God
    the morning sun will break upon us,
to shine on those who dwell in darkness
    and the shadow of death,
and to guide our feet in the way of peace.

This is a short prayer of praise that Christians sometimes add at the end of psalms. It's also part of the rosary. But it can be prayed anytime by itself, too.

The Doxology

Glory to the Father
and to the Son
and to the Holy Spirit:
as it was in the beginning,
is now, and will be for ever.
Amen.

In Latin:

Gloria Patri et Filio et Spiritui Sancto:
Sicut erat in principio, et nunc, et semper,
et in saecula saeculorum. Amen.

My·HELP
IS·THE·LORD,
WHO·MADE·EARTH
AND·THE·HEAVENS.
THE·SUN·SHALL·NOT
HARM·YOU·BY·DAY
NOR·THE·MOON
AT·NIGHT.

EVENING PRAYERS

EVENING PRAYERS

*This short prayer, adapted from two verses
of Psalm 70, is used to begin the church's daily
prayer, the Liturgy of the Hours, at all times
except morning.*

O God, come to my assistance.
O Lord, make haste to help me.

Sung at evening, this psalm proclaims that God never grows tired, but watches and keeps us safe.

Psalm 121

I lift up my eyes to the hills—
    from where does my help come?
My help comes from the Lord,
    who made heaven and earth.
The Lord will not let your foot be moved,
    the Lord who keeps you will not slumber.
The One who keeps Israel
    will neither slumber nor sleep.
The Lord is your keeper;
    the Lord is your shade
    on your right hand.
The sun shall not strike you by day,
    nor the moon by night.
The Lord will keep you from all evil,
    and will keep your life.
The Lord will keep
    your going out and your coming in
    from this time forth and for evermore.

This canticle is from the Gospel of Luke, chapter 1. Mary sang it when Elizabeth blessed her at the Visitation. Down through the ages, Mary's song of praise and liberation has been sung by the church when the sun sets.

The Song of Mary

My soul magnifies the Lord,
   and my spirit rejoices in God my Savior
who has looked with favor on me,
   a lowly serving maid.
From this day all generations
   will call me blessed.
The Mighty One has done great things for me:
   holy the name of the Lord,
whose mercy is on the God-fearing
   from generation to generation.
The arm of the Lord is filled with strength,
   scattering the proudhearted.
God cast the mighty from their thrones,
   lifting up the lowly.

God filled the hungry with good things,
    sending the rich away empty.
God has come to the help of Israel,
    the Lord's servant,
remembering mercy,
    the mercy promised to our forebears,
to Abraham and his children for ever.

*This prayer, the people's part of the great
eucharistic prayer of the Mass, is made up of
verses from the Book of Isaiah (chapter 6) and
Psalm 118. While not particularly associated
with evening, it makes a good prayer as day turns
into night. It could be prayed at any time, though.*

Holy, Holy

Holy, holy, holy Lord,
God of power and might!
Heaven and earth are full of your glory.
Hosanna in the highest!
Blessed is he who comes
in the name of the Lord!
Hosanna in the highest!

In Latin:

Sanctus, sanctus, sanctus
Dominus Deus Sabaoth.
Pleni sunt caeli et terra gloria tua.
Hosanna in excelsis!
Benedictus qui venit in nomine Domini.
Hosanna in excelsis!

I·AM·CALM
AND·TRANQUIL
LIKE·A·WEANED
CHILD
RESTING·IN·ITS
MOTHER'S·ARMS:
MY·WHOLE·BEING
AT·REST.

NIGHT PRAYERS

NIGHT PRAYERS

*This short verse from the church's daily prayer,
the Liturgy of the Hours, is a fitting way to end
the day, accompanied with the sign of the cross.*

May Almighty God give us a restful night
and a peaceful death.

Psalm 131

O Lord, my heart is not lifted up,
    my eyes are not raised too high;
I do not occupy myself with things
    too great and too marvelous for me.
But I have calmed and quieted my life,
    like a weaned child with its mother;
    I am like a weaned child.
O Israel, hope in the Lord
    now and forever.

This canticle is from the Gospel of Luke, chapter 2. It is the last biblical song that the church sings each day.

The Song of Simeon

Lord, let now your servant go in peace,
     according to your word.
My own eyes have seen the salvation
which you have prepared
     in the sight of all peoples:
     a light of revelation to the nations
and the glory of your people Israel.

*From medieval times, the final prayer of the day
is to the Mother of God. Like a mother, God will
watch and protect us as we sleep.*

Hail, Holy Queen!

Hail, holy Queen, mother of mercy,
   hail, our life, our sweetness, and our hope!
To you we cry, the children of Eve;
   to you we send up our sighs,
   mourning and weeping in this land of exile.
Turn, then, most gracious advocate,
   your eyes of mercy toward us;
   lead us home at last
   and show us the blessed fruit
   of your womb, Jesus:
O clement, O loving, O sweet Virgin Mary!

SING·TO·THE
LORD·A·NEW
SONG, 🌿🌿🌿
THE·LORD·OF
WONDERFUL
DEEDS. 🌿🌿🌿
RIGHT·HAND
AND·HOLY·ARM
BROUGHT 🌿🌿
VICTORY·TO
GOD. 🌿🌿🌿🌿

PSALMS FOR THE SEASONS OF THE CHURCH YEAR

PSALMS FOR THE SEASONS OF THE CHURCH YEAR

Advent is the four weeks before Christmas, when we prepare for Christ's second coming in glory and remember his first coming in humility.

A Psalm for Advent

Who shall ascend the hill of the Lord?
　　And who shall stand in God's holy place?
Those who have clean hands and pure hearts,
　　Who do not set their minds on falsehood,
　　and do not swear deceitfully.
They will receive blessing from the Lord,
　　and vindication from the God of their salvation.
Such is the generation of those who seek the Lord,
　　who seek the face of the God of Jacob.

Lift up your heads, O gates!
    and be lifted up, O ancient doors!
    that the Ruler of glory may come in.
Who is the Ruler of glory?
    The Lord, strong and mighty,
    The Lord, mighty in battle!
Lift up your heads, O gates!
    and be lifted up, O ancient doors!
    that the Ruler of glory may come in.
Who is this Ruler of glory?
    The Lord of hosts,
    the Lord is the Ruler of glory!

—*Psalm 24:3–10*

Christmas is a season, not just a day! It begins at sunset on December 24 and lasts until we celebrate the feast of the Baptism of the Lord in January.

A Psalm for Christmastime

O sing to the Lord a new song,
    for the Lord has done marvelous things!
God's right hand and holy arm
    have gotten the victory,
The Lord has declared victory,
    and has revealed vindication in the sight
    of the nations.
The Lord has remembered steadfast love
    and faithfulness
    to the house of Israel.
All the ends of the earth have seen
    the victory of our God.

Make a joyful noise to the Lord, all the earth;
  break forth into joyous song and sing praises!
Sing praises to the Lord with the lyre,
  with the lyre and the sound of melody!
With trumpets and the sound of the horn
  make a joyful noise before the Ruler, the Lord!

Let the sea roar, and all that fills it;
  the world and those who dwell in it!
Let the floods clap their hands;
  let the hills sing for joy together
  before the Lord,
Who comes to judge the earth.
  The Lord will judge the world with
  its righteousness,
  and the peoples with equity.

—*Psalm 98*

*Lent is the church's springtime, the forty days
before the Three Holy Days of the Lord's Passion,
Death and Resurrection. We pray this psalm
of sorrow as we fast and share what we have with
the poor, in order to prepare ourselves to receive
new life in the church at Easter, when the
sacraments of baptism, confirmation and
eucharist are celebrated.*

A Psalm for Lent

Have mercy on me, O God,
    according to your steadfast love;
According to your abundant mercy
    blot out my transgressions.
Wash me thoroughly from my iniquity,
    and cleanse me from my sin!
For I know my transgressions,
    and my sin is ever before me.
Against you, you only, I have sinned,
    and done that which is evil in your sight,
so that you are justified in your sentence
    and blameless in your judgment.

Indeed, I was born into iniquity,
    and I have been sinful
    since my mother conceived me.

Surely, you desire truth in the inward being;
    therefore teach me wisdom in my secret heart.
Purge me with hyssop, and I shall be clean;
    wash me, and I shall be whiter than snow;
Let me hear with joy and gladness;
    let the bones which you have broken rejoice.
Hide your face from my sins,
    and blot out all my iniquities.

Create in me a clean heart, O God,
    And put a new and right spirit within me.
Cast me not away from your presence,
    And take not your holy spirit from me.
Restore to me the joy of your salvation,
    And sustain in me a willing spirit.
Then I will teach transgressors your ways,
    And sinners will return to you.

—*Psalm 51:3–15*

Easter is a season of 50 days, days of singing
"Alleluia!"

A Psalm for Eastertime

O give thanks to the Lord, who is good;
    whose steadfast love endures forever!
Let Israel say,
    "God's steadfast love endures forever."
Let the house of Aaron say,
    "God's steadfast love endures forever."
Let those who fear the Lord say,
    "God's steadfast love endures forever."

I was pushed hard, so that I was falling,
    but the Lord helped me.
The Lord is my strength and my power;
    the Lord has become my salvation.
There are joyous songs of victory
    in the tents of the righteous:
"The right hand of the Lord does valiantly,
    the right hand of the Lord is exalted,
    the right hand of the Lord does valiantly!"
I shall not die, but I shall live,
    and recount the deeds of the Lord.

The stone which the builders rejected
    has become the cornerstone.
This is the Lord's doing;
    it is marvelous in our eyes.
This is the day which the Lord has made;
    let us rejoice and be glad in it.

Save us, we beseech you, O Lord!
    O Lord, we beseech you, give us success!
Blessed is the one who comes in the name
    of the Lord!
    we bless you from the house of the Lord.
The Lord is God,
    who has given us light.
Lead the festal procession with branches,
    up to the horns of the altar!
You are my God, and I will give thanks to you;
    you are my God, I will extol you.
O give thanks to the Lord, who is good;
    for God's steadfast love endures forever!

—*Psalm 118:1–4, 13–17, 22–29*

The season of Easter ends with Pentecost, the day of wind and of fire, of seven gifts and a new community. The verse beginning, "These all look to you" can also be memorized and used as a meal prayer.

A Psalm for Pentecost

Bless the Lord, O my soul!
　　O Lord my God, you are very great!
You are clothed with honor and majesty,
　　and wrapped in light as with a garment;
You stretch out the heavens like a tent,
　　and lay the beams of your chambers
　　on the waters;
You make the clouds your chariot,
　　and ride on the wings of the wind;
You make the winds your messengers,
　　fire and flame your ministers.
You set the earth on its foundations,
　　so that it shall never be shaken.
You covered it with the deep as with a garment;
　　the waters stood above the mountains.

At your rebuke they fled;
　　at the sound of your thunder
　　they fled in terror.
They rose up to the mountains,
　　ran down to the valleys,
　　to the place which you appointed for them.
You set a boundary which they cannot pass,
　　so that they might not again cover the earth.

You cause the grass to grow for cattle,
　　and plants for people to use,
　　to bring forth food from the earth,
Wine to gladden the human heart,
　　oil to make the face shine,
　　and bread to strengthen the human heart.
The trees of the Lord are watered abundantly,
　　the cedars of Lebanon that God planted.

These all look to you,
    to give them their food in due season.
When you give it to them, they gather it.
    when you open your hand, they are filled
    with good things.
When you hide your face, they are dismayed;
    when you take away their breath, they die
    and return to their dust.
When you send forth your spirit, they
    are created;
    and you renew the face of the earth.

—Psalm 104:1–9, 14–16, 27–30

HAIL, ·MARY,
FULL·OF·GRACE!
THE·LORD
IS·WITH·YOU.
BLESSED·ARE·YOU
AMONG·WOMEN,
AND·BLESSED
IS·THE·FRUIT
OF·YOUR·WOMB,
JESUS.

PRAYERS TO THE MOTHER OF GOD

Prayers to the Mother of God

The first two lines of this prayer are the words of the angel Gabriel to Mary, when he announces that she is with child (Luke 1:28). The second two lines are the words of Elizabeth's greeting to Mary, when both are with child (Luke 1:42). The last four lines come to us from deep in history, from where and from whom we do not know.

The Hail Mary

Hail, Mary, full of grace,
The Lord is with you!
Blessed are you among women,
and blessed is the fruit of your womb, Jesus.

Holy Mary, Mother of God,
pray for us sinners,
now and at the hour of our death.
Amen.

In Latin:

Ave Maria, gratia plena,
Dominus tecum,
benedicta tu in mulieribus,
et benedictus fructus ventris tui, Jesus.

Sancta Maria, Mater Dei,
ora pro nobis peccatoribus,
nunc et in hora mortis nostrae.
Amen.

This prayer is often said at noon and at six in the evening, and sometimes church bells ring to remind us. It can be prayed in parts: "V" is the verse that the leader says and "R" is the response that all make. The "Hail Mary" is on page 42. The Angelus reminds us that God became a human being, taking on our flesh and redeeming us, body and soul. It's customary to bow when you come to the words, "And the Word became flesh."

The Angelus

V. The angel spoke God's message to Mary,

R. **and she conceived of the Holy Spirit.**

V. Hail, Mary . . .

R. **Holy Mary . . .**

V. "I am the lowly servant of the Lord:

R. **let it be done to me according to your word."**

V. Hail, Mary . . .

R. **Holy Mary . . .**

V. And the Word became flesh
R. **and lived among us.**
V. Hail, Mary . . .
R. **Holy Mary . . .**
V. Pray for us, holy Mother of God,
R. **that we may become worthy of the promises of Christ.**

Let us pray.

Lord,
fill our hearts with your grace:
once, through the message of an angel
you revealed to us the incarnation of your Son;
now, through his suffering and death
lead us to the glory of his resurrection.

We ask this through Christ our Lord.

R. **Amen.**

This prayer is ascribed to Saint Bernard, a holy monk who lived in the 12th century. The Latin name means "Remember."

The Memorare

Remember, most loving Virgin Mary,
never was it heard
That anyone who turned to you for help
was left unaided.

Inspired by this confidence,
though burdened by my sins,
I run to your protection
for you are my mother.

Mother of the Word of God,
do not despise my words of pleading
but be merciful and hear my prayer.
Amen.

The Rosary

The rosary is a prayer in which we repeat the words of prayers that we know by heart in order to free our minds to meditate on the mysteries of our faith. The basic prayers of the rosary are:

    the Apostles' Creed (page 80)
    the Lord's Prayer (page 4)
    the Hail Mary (page 42)
    the Glory Be (The Doxology, page 18).

The diagram on page 49 shows how to use the beads to say the prayers.

The origins of the rosary are complex. Some ascribe it to certain holy people of past ages. Some say that when most people were illiterate and therefore could not read the 150 psalms, the rosary was devised so that one could pray 150 Hail Marys, keeping count on the beads. The beads are strung in "decades" of ten. A rosary contains five decades of ten beads. There are three sets of mysteries. So 5 decades times 10 Hail Marys is 50, said three times is 150 Hail Marys, one for each psalm in the Book of Psalms.

Many religious traditions use strings of beads as an aid to prayer. The rosary's beads are connected to a cross, the sign of Christ. The name "rosary" comes from medieval times, and refers to the prayers as a bouquet or garden of roses. The rose was a sign of the Virgin Mary.

The mysteries of the rosary are based in scripture. Before each decade, you can read the scripture passage. Each decade begins with the prayer Jesus taught us, the Our Father, and ends with the Doxology. As your fingers pass over the beads and your lips murmur the words of the prayers, your mind is free to recall the scripture story and ponder it.

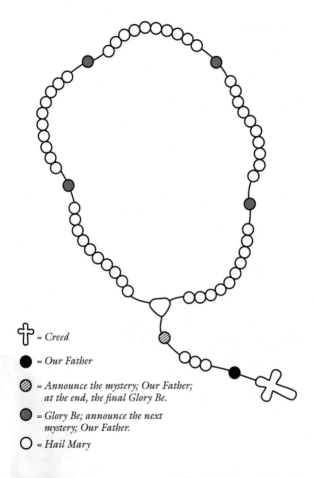

✝ = *Creed*

● = *Our Father*

◐ = *Announce the mystery; Our Father; at the end, the final Glory Be.*

◉ = *Glory Be; announce the next mystery; Our Father.*

○ = *Hail Mary*

The Joyful Mysteries

The Annunciation (Luke 1:30–33)
The Visitation (Luke 1:50–53)
The Nativity (Luke 2:10–11)
The Presentation (Luke 2:29–32)
The Finding of Jesus in the Temple (Luke 2:48–52)

The Sorrowful Mysteries

The Agony in the Garden (Matthew 26:38–39)
The Scourging at the Pillar (John 19:1)
The Crowning with Thorns (Mark 15:16–17)
The Carrying of the Cross (John 19:17)
The Crucifixion (John 19:28–30)

The Glorious Mysteries

The Resurrection (Mark 16:6–8)
The Ascension (Acts 1:10–11)
The Coming of the Holy Spirit (Acts 2:1–4)
The Assumption of Mary (Song of Songs 2:3–6)
The Coronation of Mary (Luke 1:51–54)

HOUSE • OF • GOD.
GATE • OF • HEAVEN.
DESIRE • OF • THE
ETERNAL • HILLS.
MYSTICAL • ROSE.
TOWER • OF • IVORY.
MORNING • STAR.
TERROR • OF
EVIL • SPIRITS.

LITANIES

LITANIES

Litanies are meditative prayers that focus on names: for Jesus, for Mary, for Joseph, for all the saints. We call out the name and ask "pray for us!" or "have mercy on us!" If the litany is prayed together, one person sings or calls out the name, and all respond. The litany is great to use while walking. Pay attention to your breathing: Breathe in on the name. Hold your breath for a moment. Breathe out on the response. Walk in time with the names.

Litany of the Sacred Heart of Jesus

Lord, have mercy.	**Lord, have mercy.**
Christ, have mercy.	**Christ, have mercy.**
Lord, have mercy.	**Lord, have mercy.**

God our Father in Heaven	**have mercy on us.**
God the Son, Redeemer of the world	**have mercy on us.**
God the Holy Spirit	**have mercy on us.**

Holy Trinity, one God	**have mercy on us.**
Heart of Jesus, Son of the eternal Father	**have mercy on us.**
Heart of Jesus, formed by the Holy Spirit in the womb of the Virgin Mother	**have mercy on us.**
Heart of Jesus, one with the eternal Word	**have mercy on us.**
Heart of Jesus, infinite in majesty	**have mercy on us.**
Heart of Jesus, holy temple of God	**have mercy on us.**

Heart of Jesus,
tabernacle of the
Most High   **have mercy on us.**
Heart of Jesus, house
of God and gate
of heaven   **have mercy on us.**

Heart of Jesus, aflame
with love for us   **have mercy on us.**
Heart of Jesus, source
of justice and love   **have mercy on us.**
Heart of Jesus, full of
goodness and love   **have mercy on us.**
Heart of Jesus, well-
spring of all virtue   **have mercy on us.**
Heart of Jesus, worthy
of all praise   **have mercy on us.**
Heart of Jesus, king
and center of all hearts **have mercy on us.**
Heart of Jesus,
treasure-house
of wisdom
and knowledge   **have mercy on us.**

Heart of Jesus, in
whom there dwells
the fullness of God **have mercy on us.**
Heart of Jesus, in
whom the Father
is well pleased **have mercy on us.**
Heart of Jesus, from
whose fullness we
have all received **have mercy on us.**
Heart of Jesus, desire
of the eternal hills **have mercy on us.**
Heart of Jesus, patient
and full of mercy **have mercy on us.**
Heart of Jesus,
generous to all
who turn to you **have mercy on us.**
Heart of Jesus, fountain
of life and holiness **have mercy on us.**
Heart of Jesus,
atonement for our sins **have mercy on us.**
Heart of Jesus,
overwhelmed
with insults **have mercy on us.**

Heart of Jesus, broken
for our sins **have mercy on us.**
Heart of Jesus,
obedient
even unto death **have mercy on us.**
Heart of Jesus, pierced
by a lance **have mercy on us.**
Heart of Jesus, source
of all consolation **have mercy on us.**
Heart of Jesus, our life
and resurrection **have mercy on us.**
Heart of Jesus, our
peace and reconciliation **have mercy on us.**
Heart of Jesus, victim
for our sins **have mercy on us.**
Heart of Jesus,
salvation of all
who trust in you **have mercy on us.**
Heart of Jesus, hope of
all who die in you **have mercy on us.**
Heart of Jesus, delight
of all the saints **have mercy on us.**

Lamb of God, you take
away the sins of
the world   **have mercy on us.**
Lamb of God, you take
away the sins of
the world   **have mercy on us.**
Lamb of God, you take
away the sins of
the world   **have mercy on us.**

V. Jesus, gentle and humble of heart:
R. **Touch our hearts
and make them like your own.**

Let us pray.

Father,
We rejoice in the gifts of love
we have received from the heart of Jesus,
your Son.
Open our hearts to share his life
and continue to bless us with his love.
We ask this in the name of Jesus the Lord.

Amen.

Litany of the Blessed Virgin Mary

Lord, have mercy. **Lord, have mercy.**
Christ, have mercy. **Christ, have mercy.**
Lord, have mercy. **Lord, have mercy.**

God our Father in Heaven **have mercy on us.**
God the Son, Redeemer
 of the world **have mercy on us.**
God the Holy Spirit **have mercy on us.**
Holy Trinity, one God **have mercy on us.**

Holy Mary **pray for us.**
Holy Mother of God **pray for us.**
Most honored of virgins **pray for us.**

Mother of Christ **pray for us.**
Mother of the Church **pray for us.**
Mother of divine grace **pray for us.**
Mother most pure **pray for us.**
Mother of chaste love **pray for us.**
Mother and virgin **pray for us.**
Sinless Mother **pray for us.**

Dearest of mothers	**pray for us.**
Model of motherhood	**pray for us.**
Mother of good counsel	**pray for us.**
Mother of our Creator	**pray for us.**
Mother of our Savior	**pray for us.**
Virgin most wise	**pray for us.**
Virgin rightly praised	**pray for us.**
Virgin rightly renowned	**pray for us.**
Virgin most powerful	**pray for us.**
Virgin gentle in mercy	**pray for us.**
Faithful Virgin	**pray for us.**
Mirror of justice	**pray for us.**
Throne of wisdom	**pray for us.**
Cause of our joy	**pray for us.**
Shrine of the Spirit	**pray for us.**
Glory of Israel	**pray for us.**
Vessel of selfless devotion	**pray for us.**
Mystical Rose	**pray for us.**
Tower of David	**pray for us.**
Tower of ivory	**pray for us.**
House of gold	**pray for us.**
Ark of the covenant	**pray for us.**

Gate of heaven	**pray for us.**
Morning Star	**pray for us.**
Health of the sick	**pray for us.**
Refuge of sinners	**pray for us.**
Comfort of the troubled	**pray for us.**
Help of Christians	**pray for us.**
Queen of angels	**pray for us.**
Queen of patriarchs and prophets	**pray for us.**
Queen of apostles and martyrs	**pray for us.**
Queen of confessors and virgins	**pray for us.**
Queen of all saints	**pray for us.**
Queen conceived without sin	**pray for us.**
Queen assumed into heaven	**pray for us.**
Queen of the rosary	**pray for us.**
Queen of peace	**pray for us.**

Lamb of God, you take
   away the sins of
   the world   **have mercy on us.**
Lamb of God, you take
   away the sins of
   the world   **have mercy on us.**
Lamb of God, you take
   away the sins of
   the world   **have mercy on us.**

V. Pray for us, holy Mother of God.
R. **That we may become worthy of the
promises of Christ.**

Let us pray.

Eternal God,
let your people enjoy constant health
in mind and body.
Through the intercession of the Virgin Mary
free us from the sorrows of this life
and lead us to happiness in the life to come.
Grant this through Christ our Lord.

Amen.

Litany of Saint Joseph

Lord, have mercy.   **Lord, have mercy.**
Christ, have mercy.   **Christ, have mercy.**
Lord, have mercy.   **Lord, have mercy.**

Holy Mary   **pray for us.**
Saint Joseph   **pray for us.**
Noble son of the House
    of David   **pray for us.**
Light of patriarchs   **pray for us.**
Husband of the Mother
    of God   **pray for us.**
Guardian of the Virgin   **pray for us.**
Foster father of the Son
    of God   **pray for us.**
Faithful guardian of Christ   **pray for us.**
Head of the holy family   **pray for us.**
Joseph, chaste and just   **pray for us.**
Joseph, prudent and brave   **pray for us.**
Joseph, obedient and loyal   **pray for us.**
Pattern of patience   **pray for us.**
Lover of poverty   **pray for us.**
Model of workers   **pray for us.**

Example to parents	**pray for us.**
Guardian of virgins	**pray for us.**
Pillar of family life	**pray for us.**
Comfort of the troubled	**pray for us.**
Hope of the sick	**pray for us.**
Patron of the dying	**pray for us.**
Terror of evil spirits	**pray for us.**
Protector of the Church	**pray for us.**

Lamb of God, you take away the sins of the world	**have mercy on us.**
Lamb of God, you take away the sins of the world	**have mercy on us.**
Lamb of God, you take away the sins of the world	**have mercy on us.**

V. God made him master of his household.

R. **And put him in charge of all that he owned.**

Let us pray.

Almighty God,
in your infinite wisdom and love
you chose Joseph to be the husband of Mary,
the mother of your Son.
As we enjoy his protection on earth
may we have the help of his prayers in heaven.
We ask this through Christ our Lord.

Amen.

The Litany of the Saints is prayed by the whole church whenever we baptize someone, ordain someone or wait at the side of one who is dying.

Litany of the Saints

Lord, have mercy.	**Lord, have mercy.**
Christ, have mercy.	**Christ, have mercy.**
Lord, have mercy.	**Lord, have mercy.**

Holy Mary, Mother of God	**pray for us.**
Saint Michael	**pray for us.**
Holy angels of God	**pray for us.**
Saint John the Baptist	**pray for us.**
Saint Joseph	**pray for us.**
Saint Peter and Saint Paul	**pray for us.**
Saint Andrew	**pray for us.**
Saint John	**pray for us.**
Saint Mary Magdalene	**pray for us.**
Saint Stephen	**pray for us.**
Saint Ignatius of Antioch	**pray for us.**
Saint Lawrence	**pray for us.**
Saint Perpetua and Saint Felicity	**pray for us.**

Saint Agnes	**pray for us.**
Saint Gregory	**pray for us.**
Saint Augustine	**pray for us.**
Saint Athanasius	**pray for us.**
Saint Basil	**pray for us.**
Saint Martin	**pray for us.**
Saint Benedict	**pray for us.**
Saint Francis and Saint Dominic	**pray for us.**
Saint Francis Xavier	**pray for us.**
Saint John Vianney	**pray for us.**
Saint Catherine	**pray for us.**
Saint Teresa	**pray for us.**
(other names of saints may be added.)	**(pray for us.)**
All holy men and women	**pray for us.**
Lord, be merciful	**Lord, save your people.**
From all evil	**Lord, save your people.**
From every sin	**Lord, save your people.**
From everlasting death	**Lord, save your people.**

By your coming
   as man   **Lord, save your people.**
By your death and
   rising to new life   **Lord, save your people.**
By your gift
   of the Holy Spirit **Lord, save your people.**

Be merciful to
   us sinners   **Lord, hear our prayer.**
Guide and protect
   your holy Church   **Lord, hear our prayer.**
Keep the pope and
   all the clergy
   in faithful service
   to your Church   **Lord, hear our prayer.**
Bring all peoples
   together in trust
   and peace   **Lord, hear our prayer.**
Strengthen us in
   your service   **Lord, hear our prayer.**
Jesus, Son of
   the living God   **Lord, hear our prayer.**
Christ, hear us   **Christ, hear us.**

Lord Jesus,
hear our prayer   **Lord Jesus, hear our prayer.**

Let us pray.

God of our ancestors
who set their hearts on you,
of those who fell asleep in peace,
and of those who won the martyrs'
    violent crown:
We are surrounded by these witnesses
as by clouds of fragrant incense.
In this age we would be counted
in this communion of all the saints;
keep us always in their good
and blessed company.
In their midst we make every prayer
through Christ
who is our Lord for ever and ever.

Amen.

PRAYERS TO THE HOLY SPIRIT

This prayer can be prayed with others, with the leader taking the verses marked "V" and the others making the responses marked "R." Praying to the Holy Spirit is especially appropriate on the nine days between Ascension Thursday and Pentecost Sunday, when Mary and the disciples were gathered in fervent prayer awaiting the coming of the Holy Spirit as the Risen Lord had promised them.

Come, Holy Spirit

V. Come, Holy Spirit, fill the hearts of your faithful.

R. **And kindle in them the fire of your love.**

V. Send forth your Spirit, and they shall be created.

R. **And you will renew the face of the earth.**

Let us pray.

Lord,
by the light of the Holy Spirit
you have taught the hearts of your faithful.
In the same Spirit
help us to relish what is right
and always rejoice in your consolation.
We ask this through Christ our Lord.

Amen.

This prayer, called a sequence, is sung on the day of Pentecost at Mass, between the second reading and the Alleluia before the gospel. In Latin, its title is Veni Sancte Spiritus, *or Come, Holy Spirit.*

Holy Spirit, Lord Divine,
Come, from heights of heav'n and shine.
    Come with blessed radiance bright!
Come, O Father of the poor,
Come, whose treasured gifts endure.
    Come, our heart's unfailing light!

Of consolers, wisest, best,
And our souls' most welcome guest,
    Sweet refreshment, sweet repose.
In our labor rest most sweet,
Pleasant coolness in the heat,
    Consolation in our woes.

Light most blessed, shine with grace
In our heart's most secret place,
    Fill your faithful through and through!
Left without your presence here,
Life itself would disappear,
    Nothing thrives apart from you!

Cleanse our soiled hearts of sin,
Arid souls refresh within,
    Wounded lives to health restore!
Bend the stubborn heart and will,
Melt the frozen, warm the chill,
    Guide the wayward home once more!

On the faithful who are true
And profess their faith in you,
    In your sev'n-fold gift descend!
Give us virtue's sure reward,
Give us your salvation, Lord,
    Give us joys that never end! Amen.

PRAYERS OF SAINTS

This prayer is attributed to Saint Francis of Assisi, who lived from 1181 or 1182 until 1226. It is a good prayer to pray on New Year's Day, on the anniversary of your baptism, or when you experience strife. We remember Saint Francis every year on October 4. The central insight of this prayer—that it is in dying that we are born to eternal life—is the central mystery of faith, the paschal mystery.

Prayer of Saint Francis

Lord, make me an instrument of your peace:
where there is hatred, let me sow love;
where there is injury, pardon;
where there is doubt, faith;
where there is despair, hope;
where there is darkness, light;
where there is sadness, joy.

O divine Master, grant that I may not
    so much seek
to be consoled as to console,
to be understood as to understand,
to be loved as to love.
For it is in giving that we receive,
it is in pardoning that we are pardoned,
it is in dying that we are born to eternal life.
Amen.

Here is a prayer attributed to Saint Patrick
(389–461), who brought the gospel to Ireland.
It is a reminder to live each moment aware of
God's presence. We remember Saint Patrick every
year on March 17.

Prayer of Saint Patrick

Christ be with me, Christ before me,
    Christ behind me,
Christ within me, Christ beneath me,
    Christ above me,
Christ on my right, Christ on my left,
Christ where I lie, Christ where I sit,
    Christ where I arise,
Christ in the heart of every one
    who thinks of me,
Christ in every eye that sees me,
Christ in every ear that hears me.
    Salvation is of the Lord.
    Salvation is of the Christ.
    May your salvation, O Lord, be ever with us.

PRAYERS OF SORROW

This prayer of sorrow is often used when celebrating the sacrament of penance. It is good to use at noontime and at bedtime, after briefly reflecting on how our struggle to be holy has gone thus far.

An Act of Contrition

My God,
I am sorry for my sins with all my heart.
In choosing to do wrong
    and failing to do good,
I have sinned against you
    whom I should love above all things.
I firmly intend, with your help,
    to do penance,
    to sin no more,
    and to avoid whatever leads me to sin.
Our Savior Jesus Christ
    suffered and died for us.
In his name, my God, have mercy.

Here is another prayer of sorrow, prayed by the blind man who called out to Jesus, who healed him. Don't hesitate to repeat this prayer over and over.

The Jesus Prayer

Lord Jesus, Son of God,
have mercy on me, a sinner.

This chant, used at times in the Mass, was originally prayed in Greek, even when the Mass was first translated into the language of the people—at that time, Latin.

Kyrie eleison

Lord have mercy.
Christ have mercy.
Lord have mercy.

In Greek:

Kyrie eleison.
Christe eleison.
Kyrie eleison.

This chant is sung at Mass at the breaking of the bread, addressed to Jesus. The first two verses can be repeated over and over again, but the last verse always ends "grant us peace."

Lamb of God

Lamb of God,
you take away the sins of the world,
have mercy on us!

Lamb of God,
you take away the sins of the world,
have mercy on us!

Lamb of God,
you take away the sins of the world,
grant us peace!

In Latin:

Agnus Dei,
qui tollis peccata mundi,
misere nobis!

Agnus Dei,
qui tollis peccata mundi,
misere nobis!

Agnus Dei,
qui tollis peccata mundi,
dona nobis pacem!

*The best psalm of sorrow is Psalm 51, found on
page 34.*

ETERNAL·REST
GRANT·UNTO·THEM,
O·LORD,
AND·LET
PERPETUAL·LIGHT
SHINE·UPON·THEM.
MAY·THEY
REST·IN·PEACE.
MAY·THE·SOULS
OF·ALL·THE
FAITHFUL·DEPARTED
THROUGH·THE
MERCY·OF·GOD,
REST·IN·PEACE.

PRAYERS FOR THE DEAD

PRAYERS FOR THE DEAD

This prayer can be prayed with others: The "V" is the leader's verse and the "R" is the response that all make. It is used at the end of the vigil, the first part of a funeral. It can be prayed for an individual, by inserting his or her name, or for all the dead. It is especially good to pray this prayer in November, when we remember all the saints and souls of those who have died, and whenever visiting or even passing by a cemetery.

Eternal Rest

V. Eternal rest grant unto
   [*Name*/him/her/them], O Lord,
R. **and let perpetual light
   shine upon [him/her/them].**

V. May [he/she/they] rest in peace.
R. **Amen.**

V. May [his/her/their] soul(s), and the souls
   of all the faithful departed,
   through the mercy of God, rest in peace.
R. **Amen.**

This ancient song is sung as a final song of loving farewell at the end of the second part of the Christian funeral, the funeral liturgy.

In Paradise

May the angels lead you into paradise;
may the martyrs come to welcome you
and take you to the holy city,
the new and eternal Jerusalem.
May the choirs of angels welcome you,
and where Lazarus is poor no longer
may you find eternal rest.

In Latin:

In paradisum deducant te angeli:
in tuo adventu suscipiant te martyres,
et perducant te in civitatem sanctam Jerusalem.
Chorus angelorum te suscipiat,
et cum Lazaro quondam paupere
aeternam habeas requiem.

I BELIEVE·IN
GOD·THE·FATHER.
I·BELIEVE·IN
JESUS·CHRIST.
I·BELIEVE·IN
THE·HOLY·SPIRIT
IN·THE·HOLY
CATHOLIC·CHURCH.

CREEDS AND VOWS

CREEDS AND VOWS

Creeds are not exactly prayers addressed to God,
but proclamations of faith made before God.

The Apostles' Creed

I believe in God, the Father almighty,
    creator of heaven and earth.
I believe in Jesus Christ, his only Son,
    our Lord.
      He was conceived by the power
      of the Holy Spirit
      and born of the Virgin Mary.
He suffered under Pontius Pilate,
    was crucified, died, and was buried.
He descended to the dead.
On the third day he rose again.
He ascended into heaven,
    and is seated at the right hand of the Father.
He will come again
    to judge the living and the dead.

I believe in the Holy Spirit,
 the holy catholic Church,
 the communion of saints,
 the forgiveness of sins,
 the resurrection of the body,
 and the life everlasting.
Amen.

The Nicene Creed

We believe in one God,
    the Father, the Almighty,
    maker of heaven and earth,
    of all that is seen and unseen.

We believe in one Lord, Jesus Christ,
    the only Son of God,
    eternally begotten of the Father,
    God from God, Light from Light,
    true God from true God,
    begotten, not made,
    one in Being with the Father.
    Through him all things were made.
    For us men and for our salvation
    he came down from heaven:
    by the power of the Holy Spirit
    he was born of the Virgin Mary,
    and became man.

For our sake he was crucified
under Pontius Pilate;
    he suffered, died, and was buried.
    On the third day he rose again

in fulfillment of the Scriptures;
he ascended into heaven
and is seated at the right hand
of the Father.
He will come again in glory
to judge the living and the dead,
and his kingdom will have no end.

We believe in the Holy Spirit,
the Lord, the giver of life,
who proceeds from the Father and the Son.
With the Father and the Son
he is worshiped and glorified.
He has spoken through the Prophets.
We believe in one holy
catholic and apostolic Church.
We acknowledge one baptism
for the forgiveness of sins.
We look for the resurrection of the dead,
and the life of the world to come.
Amen.

*When we are baptized, these vows are made for us
or by us. Each year at Easter, we renew the vows
of our faith. You may also renew your baptismal
vows on the anniversary of your baptism each
year, blessing yourself with the sign of the cross
and holy water brought home from church.*

Renunciation of Sin and Profession of Faith

Do you reject sin so as to live in the freedom
of God's children?

I do.

Do you reject the glamour of evil and refuse
to be mastered by sin?

I do.

Do you reject Satan, father of sin and prince
of darkness?

I do.

Do you believe in God, the Father almighty,
creator of heaven and earth?

I do.

Do you believe in Jesus Christ, his only Son our Lord, who was born of the Virgin Mary, was crucified, died, and was buried, rose from the dead, and is now seated at the right hand of the Father?

I do.

Do you believe in the Holy Spirit, the holy catholic Church, the communion of saints, the forgiveness of sins, the resurrection of the body, and life everlasting?

I do.

This is our faith. This is the faith of the Church. We are proud to profess it in Christ Jesus our Lord.

Amen.

JESUS·SAID,
"WHEN·YOU·ARE
PRAYING,
DO·NOT·HEAP·UP
EMPTY·PHRASES,
FOR·YOUR
FATHER·KNOWS
WHAT·YOU·NEED
BEFORE·YOU·ASK·HIM.
PRAY·THEN
IN·THIS·WAY."

—*Matthew 6:7, 9*